Praise for
Spiritual AND Wealthy Wisdom for Grads

"Deborah has done it again! If you want to learn master secrets from *The Spiritual and Wealth Coach* and you're ready to shorten your learning curve with how to create your own successful life path, then read my friend Deborah 'Atianne' Wilson's innovative book, designed just for you."

> James Malinchak
> Featured on ABC's Hit TV Show, *Secret Millionaire*
> Two-Time National College Speaker of the Year
> Co-Author of *Chicken Soup for the College Soul*
> Founder, www.BigMoneySpeaker.com

"Having taught university-level writing courses at six different colleges over the course of nearly 14 years, I wish we could prepare students with more of *this* type of guidance. We too often teach graduates 'what it takes to succeed' from a limited scope—Deborah's essential wisdom in this book is from an unlimited yet practical place that can situate any graduate in success, joy and freedom."

> Erika M. Schreck
> Founder, Writer and Consultant, www.erikaschreck.com
> Founder, www.TurtleHealingEnergy.com
> Former Instructor, University of Colorado Boulder, University
>   of Colorado Colorado Springs, University of Wisconsin-
>   Green Bay, University of Wisconsin-Milwaukee, Cardinal
>   Stritch University, and DeVry University

Spiritual AND Wealthy
Wisdom For Grads

Also by Deborah "Atianne" Wilson

Books
It's OK to be Spiritual AND Wealthy:
19 Essential Keys for Living a
Joyful, Prosperous & Abundant Life

Jump-Start Your Success:
23 Top Speakers Share Their Insights for
Creating More Success, Wealth and Happiness

Music
Oneness Becomes You™
"Magnum Opus"
Channeled Music for Your Ascension
~ 11:11 ~
(2-CD set)

Home Study
Trust Your Heart
3 Easy Keys to Unlocking the Power of Your Intuition
and Creating a Spiritual and Wealthy Life
(4-CD set, action guide & journal,
4-CD set transcription)

Spiritual AND Wealthy
Wisdom for Grads

44 Insightful Nuggets for Creating Authentic Success

Deborah "Atianne" Wilson

WHITE HERON PUBLISHING
Boulder, Colorado

Book design: Deborah "Atianne" Wilson and Erika M. Schreck
Editing: Erika M. Schreck, www.erikaschreck.com
Proofreading: Erika M. Schreck
Cover design: Melissa Edwards, www.lemonadecreative.com

Deborah "Atianne" Wilson is not a medical doctor. This book is not intended as a substitute for the medical advice or treatment from a physician. The reader should regularly consult a physician in matters relating to his/her health and particularly with respect to any symptoms that may require diagnosis or medical attention. The intent of the author is only to offer information of a general nature to help the reader in his/her quest for holistic well-being. In the event the reader uses any of the information in this book, which is his/her constitutional and individual right, the author and the publisher assume no responsibility for the reader's actions or results.

Printed in the USA

Library of Congress Cataloging-in-Publication Data
Wilson, Deborah "Atianne"
  Spiritual and wealthy wisdom for grads: 44 insightful nuggets for creating authentic
  success / Deborah "Atianne" Wilson
        p. cm.
1. Self-Help. 2. Spirituality. 3. Body, Mind, Spirit.

ISBN-13: 978-0692460399
ISBN-10: 069246039X

WHITE HERON PUBLISHING
Boulder, Colorado

www.whiteheronpublishing.com

Dedicated to my son Bryce

*All you need to succeed is
already contained within you*

Contents

Acknowledgments

I AM and will forever be truly thankful for *it all*. All of my life experiences have always been and will continue to be an invitation to love unconditionally. Every experience has been an invitation for me to live and express my uniquely authentic life from a space of Love, while encouraging others to do the same.

When I wrote my first book, *It's OK to be Spiritual AND Wealthy*, I thought that writing a book would be something I would do alone, leaving me initially feeling overwhelmed. Thankfully, I shifted that limiting thinking and was able to allow *this* book to manifest with much more ease, grace and joy.

I am so touched by the loving souls who still continue to keep me moving forward and laughing, as well as feeling inspired and held. They also support the often mundane parts of my life like watering plants, cleaning house, and all the tasks that can take a back seat while creating something that wants to express itself through me.

Bringing this book into form is possible because I have a team of friends, family, coaches and clients who gift me with their precious time and talents, and love me no matter what.

I AM Grateful to...

The Source of All That Is, for the gifts and messages you illuminate through me, reminding me of my Divinity so that I can remind others—and for the love and humor you radiate, which continues to expand my heart and my voice.

Erika Schreck, my friend, my teacher, my book midwife. There is no other being that could have done what you have for me in bringing these *paper-filled children* to earth. In the glory of all my contrasting energy, you stay present, tender and safe, helping me to focus when I momentarily forget my own wisdom. You are priceless.

Dianna Mednick, my mother, my friend; for being the rock I can turn to, count on and laugh until I cry with. All that lives under my roof survives and thrives because of your impeccable care and your *bossy pants*. I am who I am because of the intensity of your love, your humor and your devotion.

Allen Mednick, for being the perfect space of *proud dad* that I didn't even know I needed until you shared how proud you were of me and my work when I published my first book. You have healed spaces within my heart that I will always treasure.

My Beloved Edmund, for *still being all in*, flying home, sharing morning coffee, loving me the way God loves me, healing my heart and making me feel like a comedic genius. *Soy todo tuyo.*

James Malinchak, my friend and master marketing teacher for being the answer to my prayers, showing me how to take my gifts and create a thriving business I love. I am delighted and amazed by your generous spirit and the unique way you can hover over a person's business, helping create the impact desired.

Melissa Edwards, for the ease and grace in which you shared your creative talents contributing to this book, adding nourishment to my life and practice with your trust, vulnerability and strength and, above all, the laughter and love you gift me with our friendship.

Foreword

I have dedicated my life to helping others "Achieve a Better, Richer Business and Life!"™ My strong passion for serving others has led to teaching hundreds of thousands my unique personal and business strategies through my corporate, college and youth speaking, public seminars, private coaching, books, online courses and videos, and home study courses.

Especially close to my heart is helping students create a successful future by developing the belief in themselves that they can overcome challenges and achieve their dreams and goals.

When Deborah and I discussed her first book *It's OK to be Spiritual AND Wealthy*, I knew she had guidance that needed to be shared with the world, as her practical wisdom helps people shift and increase abundance, joy and freedom in their lives. Then, she told me about this book, and I encouraged her to get it out as soon as possible.

Graduation ceremonies happen at various times in our lives, as we complete segments of our educational experiences. We celebrate, but we also can get scared of not quite knowing what's ahead; graduation can be a mixed experience as a result.

In my own work and in Deborah's work, we believe that people can be successful and achieve what they want, and they also need to realize the importance of team. We all need seasoned teachers and coaches along the way to show us what we may be missing and to cheer us on when we doubt ourselves. This book offers that brilliant guiding voice and support for your own journey.

Having worked with Deborah "Atianne" Wilson for several years, I consider her a leading authority in creating a successful life, which inspired me to have her speak several times at my public seminars. She inspires her clients and audiences to go beyond meditation and positive thinking, grounding spirituality with practicality to do things the *right* way. She is both dedicated and skilled at helping her clients get honest about where they are in their lives and what is necessary for making positive shifts for creating more freedom and happiness.

What I love about this book is that the information is delivered in succinct lessons that will empower you to create the positive future you deserve. If you truly absorb these gems of wisdom into your thoughts, feelings and actions, you can achieve any desired dreams and goals.

Read Deborah's opening chapters "An Invitation to the Graduate" and "What I Believe about YOU," as they will set the stage for understanding the mindset for creating a successful life. Then, dive in. Decide if you'd like to read the 44 insightful nuggets of wisdom sequentially or at random. Either way, trust they're all essential. This book will inspire you far beyond graduation.

Congratulations, graduate!

James Malinchak

Featured on ABC's Hit TV Show, *Secret Millionaire*
Two-Time National College Speaker of the Year
Co-Author of *Chicken Soup for the College Soul*
Founder, www.BigMoneySpeaker.com

Your Invitation

An Invitation to the Graduate

Be Yourself.

Love deeply. Speak your truth. Align your actions with your vision. Laugh. Don't take things so seriously. Cry. When you ache, remember: "this too shall pass." Be open. Be obedient to your inner voice. Heal the hearts of others with your smile, laugh, hugs and words. Laugh more. Give wildly to yourself the gifts of self-love, respect, honor, compassion and kindness. Forgive. Drink lots of water. Be responsible for your own happiness. Remember you are the cake. Let everything outside of you be the icing on your cake. Laugh even more. Trust that you know exactly what to do. See everything as a gift. Expect to see the good in yourself, others and the world.

Always remember how very loved you are~

To Your Spiritual AND Wealthy Journey,

Deborah "Atianne" Wilson

What I Believe About YOU!

I believe you are a miracle.

> *The sooner you own this, the more joyful your life will become!*

I believe you are here to uncover, discover and play in the energy of infinite possibilities and experiences that have never been done, experienced or brought forth into this plane of existence ever before.

> *You are unique, so please don't pretend to be average!*

I believe that you are good and worthy and that there is nothing wrong with you—with the exception of what you may *think* might be wrong with you.

> *You didn't arrive on earth, thinking something was wrong with you—you gathered that along the way. So, what you've gathered you can "un-gather."*

I believe you chose to be here.

> *You are not here randomly. You have always had and will always have choice.*

I believe you were chosen to be here.

> *All that created the land and the sea invited you to come play.*

I believe while you experience this human form, you are always at choice to make new agreements.

> *You are at liberty to change your mind and choose what uplifts you. Honor yourself when you are intuitively guided in a new direction.*

I believe any struggle and suffering that you experience can become gifts when you choose to discover more of who are and your Divine potential.

> *Extraordinary openings for your potential will come from pain, but they will also come from joy.*

I believe you are a sacred being.

> *It is not arrogant to know you are sacred. Everyone is. This is Grace.*

I believe you came into this world, forgetting your magnificence.

> *Your journey is to find your way back to a place of deep awareness of your collective connection and your ability to create.*

I believe this is your awakening.

> *Trust that your awakening is an on-going journey, and there is no right or wrong way to awaken.*

I believe that in your awakening and further revealing of the truth of who you are, you get to remember the vibration of creation—joy, love and freedom in all you chose.

> *You are invited to discover you have always been home and have always had the power to choose.*

I believe you knew in your invitation to play on earth that you would be on a mission to find your way home to fully express your most glorious self.

> *Everything you experience is an invitation from Love to be your most authentic, glorious self.*

I believe you knew before you came that this earthly experience was temporary and that you are eternal.

> *Your earthly life is not all there is. Quest to make meaning for all that you see and all you don't.*

I believe you thought it would be easy and fun and an adventure, from your soul's perspective.

> *There is a vast difference in how your personality reacts and how your soul reacts.*

I believe your soul always sees this life as an adventure, and any darkness to overcome is merely the *egoic* force that is ultimately your gift, in that it is your greatest opponent.

> *The light and dark are equally important; their contrast will inform your journey.*

I believe the *ego* has been perfectly placed for you to meet and subsequently overcome in your remembering who you are and what you are truly capable of.

> *Attempting to ignore or eliminate your ego is futile. Learn from it, and then triumph over it.*

I believe that it is in knowing Yourself, in remembering, in being true to Yourself and in trusting your Divine connection, you can live fully in your purpose and passions, providing even more expansion of your inner light, which serves you, others and the world.

> *Your presence here changes the world. Yes, YOU!*

**You are never alone.
You are loved.
You matter.**

44 Insightful Nuggets for
Creating Authentic Success

Any painful experience invites us
to triumph over any adversity
by shifting our beliefs,
our habits and our mindset
to create something
more extraordinary.

one

Painful experiences are not punishments; they are soulful invitations to shift and grow so that you can actually achieve your goals and heart's desire with speed and grace.

Successful people know that each painful experience they encounter presents a choice: You can either get stuck in the pain and suffering, or you can ask yourself meaningful questions that will propel you forward with more clarity, such as "What do I need to know for my highest good about this situation?"

It all matters—we all matter.

two

There is only one extraordinary, unique you. No matter what you choose to do in life, you will bring your uniqueness to your work and relationships that no one else can.

The most successful people understand and know that no matter how many people there currently are in the career they choose, or how the economy is or isn't at any given moment, *there is always room* for one more extraordinary person who can bring unique talents and willingness to succeed in any area – you are that person!

You are Love in all its forms.

three

You are in relationship with all you do and all that you encounter. When you are speaking and acting from the space of your most loving, authentic self, you are being your most sacred self—Love.

The most loving and successful people create good, solid boundaries for themselves and others, creating success from a place of alignment.

Often we allow our *egoic* thinking
to edit what we know to be true.

four

You have two voices competing for your attention. One is your critical voice, and the other is the voice of your wisest self. One will stall your progress, and one will show you how to get from where you are to where you want to be. Most people give too much time and attention to the critical voice.

Wildly successful people learn to listen and act from the wise voice within that encourages them beyond their fears and self-doubt. Your wise voice knows what is best for you. Learn to trust it, and take action from what you know is true for you.

Set your ego aside and
take action, so you can create
joy and freedom in your life.

five

Your egoic critical voice will tell you *you're not good enough* or *you're not ready* or ask, "Who are you to think you can do this?'

Tell your critical voice, "Not now," and take action towards your dream, no matter what. Successful people believe "if you have dreamt it and you can see it, then it is yours." Let nothing or no one stand in your way from moving lovingly in the direction of your dreams.

We can always regain control
of our lives when we initiate new
patterns with how we react to
circumstances outside ourselves.

six

There will be people and experiences that will surprise and may even shock you, based on your point of view, your beliefs and what you value.

Successful people accept they cannot control people or experiences and know they can only control their reactions. Ask yourself what you can learn from situations and people. Be open to learning something new about yourself and others to move forward in your success.

Look beyond your paycheck
for other ways you can attract
the energy of money.

seven

You and what you want to create are more than your paycheck, income or bank account. Creating financial freedom means different things to different people. You have an inner desire already within you about what you want to create.

You may be able to attract the money you desire with a single career choice that you love, or you may want to attract money beyond what you choose to do for work or what you intended when you attended school.

Financially successful people tend to "think outside the box" and do things like invest in real estate or create a side business. Be aware of the ways you already attract and create financial freedom now, like great deals you get while shopping or when friends treat you for lunch. It all counts!

Financial flow is unlimited.
Any limits you experience are held
within your vibration.

eight

Financially successful people learn to move past any beliefs that limit their ability to attract and receive money. First, they notice the financial results they create in their life; then, they investigate any limiting thought, feeling or action that might be sabotaging their financial flow and freedom.

Check in on your own vibration with money: What are your beliefs about money? What do you think of people with money?

By studying and learning from those who are creating wealth with spiritual alignment and integrity, you can change your current point of financial attraction.

Let go of thinking that
manifesting money into your life
must look a certain way.

nine

The Universe will always conspire with you in any area that you put the most time and attention with your thoughts, feelings and actions.

Being successful with manifesting money or anything in your life comes from the expectation of achieving your dreams while simultaneously letting go of any attachment to the ways you think your dream *should* manifest. Successful people know that when they let go of their attachments and focus solely on what they want with their thoughts, feelings and actions, they will often co-create more magical and fulfilling results than they could have ever imagined.

Be open to receive all forms
of creative cash flow and financial
freedom from the energy of Source.

ten

As you dream, intend and pray to plan exactly how your life will go, you will often be invited to fulfill your dreams with opportunities that won't look like anything like you thought they would.

As you dream and focus with consistent positive expectations and actions for your dreams, the Universe conspires every step of the way with you. Your invitation is to be open to every opportunity that presents itself and invites you to move forward in a new direction.

Successful people trust that the Universe is co-creating with them. They know that creating financial freedom entails being open to unexplainable synchronicities, surprises and "dead-ends" that create expanded opportunities to create more money in a variety of ways.

⚬⚬⚬

Your journey and all that is included in it is an invitation to remember the Unconditional Loving energy that you are.

⚬⚬⚬

eleven

Above all else, to remember the Unconditional Loving energy you are is success.

To allow *everything* within your experience to be an invitation to love is to live an extraordinary life each and every day, not just when a dream is finally realized in physical form.

Those who are *truly successful* in all areas of their life have come to know their true worth beyond bank accounts and material accumulation.

To surrender to Unconditional Love is to consciously do something extraordinary, and to do something extraordinary is your very nature.

twelve

Everyone has unique gifts—special contributions to bring to this life. When you surrender to Unconditional Love, you allow your unique and extraordinary expression to come through.

Successful people surrender to Unconditional Love and let go of misunderstandings they have taken on from other people or experiences that have left them feeling like they have nothing worthy to contribute. They are then willing to discover and allow their unique gifts, talents and abilities to serve others.

Surrendering to Unconditional Love is the ability to see and express your soul's beauty and goodness.

Conscious celebration literally
recalibrates your energetic resonance.

thirteen

Each day can present you with multiple people and experiences to celebrate. Celebration is a conscious daily practice and focus for successful people.

Successful individuals don't wait until dreams have come true or everything in their life *feels good*; even when life feels overwhelming and challenging, they consciously expect to find something to celebrate. During the most challenging times, it is especially important to find *something* to celebrate so that you can shift your feelings—your personal resonance—to a higher and more positive place.

Your Divine nature
is celebration.

fourteen

What if you woke up every day and went to sleep every night, consciously celebrating your life in some way? What if, despite any bad, sad or overwhelming day, you were able to find something to celebrate within it?

Those who know that their happiness and success are solely dependent on what they believe about life find the daily practice of celebration focuses and energizes the positive and the possible.

Being truly successful will always come from how you feel about your life, and your feelings are always generated by thoughts and beliefs. Align your thinking with the energy that created galaxies and flowers, and you will create more joy everyday.

Your *daily* practice is to be self-aware throughout your day of all the things, people and experiences that invite you to a higher perspective.

fifteen

Things don't just happen, and nothing is random. The entirety of your life can have meaning and inspiration when you allow it to. You can easily see and feel a higher perspective when people and experiences are aligned with what you believe is good and valuable. It takes courage, commitment and dedication to investigate anything that triggers you, when people and experiences *are not* aligned with what you believe is good and valuable.

Successful people don't allow themselves to get stuck and hold on to any energy that triggers them. They take the time to go within and ask meaningful questions so that they can gain a higher perspective with any situation and create a deep sense of personal freedom.

The spiritual practice of being present in the grace of gratitude includes all of our experiences—what we deem positive as well as negative.

sixteen

The most successful people learn to *Find the Gold* in experiences they initially judge and feel to be negative. An experience and how you initially feel about it are not where you focus your gratitude. The grace of gratitude comes from *Finding the Gold*, which is the higher perspective you can extract from a seemingly negative experience and what you *will do* or *not do* differently in the future.

Successful people *Find the Gold* in everything.

Pain is not a punishment; it's your soul's request to pay attention.

seventeen

The degree of emotional or physical pain can support you in creating your most successful life. When you pay attention to pain and learn to discern that it is not a punishment or karmic retribution but an opportunity to see the difference from where you are in physical form, compared to where your highest aspect sees you and is guiding you.

Successful people recognize that the most painful experiences and the people within those experiences invite them to be their most glorious selves and to live in alignment with their authenticity and dreams. It is from this place that success lives and can expand in your life.

Refuse to settle for chronically feeling miserable, angry, resentful or hurt.

eighteen

Unhappy feelings are just as important as our happiest ones. All emotions give us feedback about what we think and then feel about any given situation. Remember that you always have a choice to shift how you think, which will shift how you feel.

Successful people learn practical skills and tools to shift and move through painful thoughts, feelings and situations because they value the wealth of feeling better, feeling good and feeling happy. They also have learned the value of reaching out and asking for support when they feel they are unable to transform their thoughts, feelings and situation on their own. You deserve to live a happy life.

The places we can find the most gold are those places in which we also find initially the most difficult to do so.

nineteen

Do you have a philosophy to find and expect goodness, no matter what? The people who feel the happiest, healthiest and most successful create *extraordinary* from the ordinary. They also find golden wisdom and opportunities from the most unexpected and even most painful experiences.

Expect to *Find the Gold* no matter what – this philosophy can create wealth in every area of your life.

Staying stuck or devastated does
not allow for the exponential growth
and expansion of your soul—
Finding the Gold does.

twenty

Life presents a cornucopia of contrasting experiences, from the wonderful and amazing to the *how can I go on with my life*? There will be situations you can change, even if it's just changing your thoughts and perspective, but there will also be situations that you clearly can't change, like the death of a friend or family member.

Successful people continually learn that resisting the experiences of life will bring suffering at some energetic level. Successful people learn to take care of themselves, ask others for help and strive to accept what is presented. Instead of staying stuck or devastated, they excavate nuggets of wisdom that propel them forward and take action where it's appropriate and aligned.

There is *always* a new way to think, feel and act.

The more you trust yourself and your aligned inner dialogue with the Divine, the less frequently you will seek other people's opinions and approval.
This is freedom.

twenty-one

Knowing exactly what you need to do, without the need to constantly consult with others, is one of the most important aspects of your inner growth and success. Being successful takes courage and strength. It takes going against the opinions and objections of those around you — *even those you love the most.*

No one can know what is right and true for you. Successful people cultivate learning to listen, trust and take action on their own inner guidance. They simultaneously learn from the results they have created when they acted on their guidance as well as when they ignored it.

When you feel any emotional charge about letting go of unforgiveness, you are still energetically bound to that person or the experience that you are allowing to hold you back.

twenty-two

When you hold the energy of unforgiveness, you are interfering with the energetic ability to attract what you are wanting. You are also perpetuating an energetic field from within you that continues to attract more of the same painful experiences you have yet to forgive.

Successful people know that forgiveness is an on-going process of self-awareness and a key to their personal freedom. They know it ALL counts, whether it's forgiving friends, family or coworkers, or establishments like the government or a corporation. Who or what in your life needs your forgiveness so that you can move forward more freely?

You must feel your beauty;
the magnificence of
who you are will never
be truly reflected in any mirror.

twenty-three

Most people have been judged negatively by someone and impacted adversely at some level. Many of us have been allowing someone else's judgment of who we are to be our reflection. The ability to feel our magnificence, the truth of who we are, comes from letting go of painful experiences and unexpressed emotions when we permitted others to be the reflection of who we are or how we look.

Successful people take time to reflect. Reflection is a co-creative, truth-revealing experience that invites us to experience our magnificence and heal wounds that create stagnation along our journey.

Feeling your magnificence and the truth of who you really are comes from gifting yourself time to sit quietly and listen with all your senses to the energetic reflection of your Divinity.

Believe you are worthy and that
you deserve whatever you desire.

twenty-four

We form our beliefs based on consistent thoughts, but beliefs are not necessarily true just because you or others think them.

Being successful and happy is a mindset filled with knowing you are worthy *and* worthy of creating what you desire, despite anything you may have integrated from other people's limited beliefs. Successful people give up concerning themselves about what other people think and put more energy into caring more about their own beliefs and perceptions, and whether their beliefs are congruent and aligned with their desires.

Let go of any limiting beliefs
and what anyone else thinks
about you or what you desire.

twenty-five

From the moment we are born, we create stories and derive meaning from our experiences. Some of the stories we tell ourselves propel us forward, while others create blocks in our ability to manifest our desires.

When we value what other people think or how they behave toward us, we delay our ability to create the happy, successful life we desire when we allow their thoughts and beliefs to override what we know is right and true for us.

Successful people move forward with or without approval of others. They also surround themselves with like-minded people, and they give limited energy to those who disapprove or criticize.

Trust that there is Infinite Supply
and you are not taking away
from anyone else's well-being.

twenty-six

It is often difficult to grasp the idea of Infinite Supply. Often we struggle with understanding why there is such discrepancy in what some people have and what others don't. If you don't believe there is Infinite Supply, you may find it helpful to contemplate or meditate on this concept.

Infinite Supply is an invitation to *not* hold yourself back because you think that in doing so there would be more for someone else. The more you open up to blossom into your most extraordinary, healthiest, wealthiest and happiest self, you will actually have more to offer others in infinite ways. If you are *without* any material wealth, you *don't* make others wealthier. If you are unwell, you don't increase someone else's health.

Successful people know that creating health for themselves allows them the ability to go out in the world and help others. Successful people know that creating wealth for themselves at any level creates opportunities to serve others and helps others to create their own dreams.

Any time you can gain clarity
and higher meaning,
you allow more inner peace
and more prosperity.

twenty-seven

Experiences that will make little or no sense to you will be scattered throughout your life. The more painful the experience feels to you, the more likely you can get stuck in thoughts and feelings that can keep you from the success and the freedom you deserve.

You may find yourself asking "why"-focused questions. For example, maybe you've asked, "Why did this happen? If I just knew *why* this happened, I'd be okay, and I could get through this and move on." Questions like these are often futile and perpetuate more negative feelings because you're coming from the level of *egoic* victim consciousness. What you're actually looking for is higher meaning, requiring a different approach.

Successful people actively extract deeper meaning from their experiences. Instead of asking "why"-based questions, two questions that you can play with and contemplate are "What might <insert person's name>'s positive intention be in this situation?" and "What do I need to know for my highest good about _____?"

When we ask for help,
we innately know a solution exists.

twenty-eight

Our soul knows we have unlimited possibilities and infinite solutions. Creating a successful life involves asking for support in a variety of ways. As we are internally guided to ask for help, we honor ourselves and we honor others. By asking for help, we demonstrate self-love, and we remind others to do the same.

Your ego often convinces you that you have to do everything on your own. Be courageous and ask for help, and know that asking for help is one of the most positive traits you can have to create the life of your dreams.

Successful people realize they need team to accomplish their goals. When you ask for help, you begin to heal the illusion of separation, as you step into the deeper awareness and consciousness that *we all are connected*.

You cannot continue to focus your thoughts and words on what's not working in your life and expect to create what you desire.

twenty-nine

It is Divine Law that you will create experiences and manifest from the energetic place where you focus the majority of your thoughts, feelings and actions. You can't live from a place of chronic negativity and expect to have positive results. It just won't happen.

Creating the successful and happy life you desire and deserve comes from surrounding yourself with positive people who inspire and uplift you—and not engaging in the chronic negative mindset of those who are stuck in *victim consciousness*. Consistently focus and realign your thoughts, feelings and actions to be congruent with what you want.

If you expect something to be different,
you need to declare from
the vision of *what is possible,* not
from your current results or
other people's limited beliefs.

thirty

Hold fast to your vision that you know in your heart is something that is right and true for you. Not everyone is going to agree with you or believe in your dreams, so don't let anyone or anything keep you from moving forward and creating successes. Some of the most extraordinary human endeavors, inventions and cures were initially met with ridicule, speculation and objection.

Move forward, despite your current circumstances and the objections of others. Let any previous negative results and any opposition inspire you to play bigger than you previously thought you could. Sometimes the opposition and limited beliefs from others will fuel your inner fire to succeed, despite all perceived odds.

Be willing to forgive.

thirty-one

No area in your life can be kept energetically separate from another. People who don't forgive their parents or a parent, for example, tend to experience difficulty with increasing their wealth and financial freedom. Be willing to forgive as you become aware of any negative charge you have about yourself, someone else or a past experience.

Forgiveness frees you to love and give more deeply. Forgiveness opens your energetic channels to receive, which is essential to creating EVERYTHING you desire.

Successful people know that in order to attract what they want and create success in *every area* of their lives, they need to monitor their thoughts and feelings and shift any area that holds unforgiveness to a place of loving neutrality.

The very nature of our choices is directly related to expanding our consciousness.

thirty-two

You cannot not grow or fail to expand your consciousness—but you can choose your rate of growth and how you experience it. Every choice you make *and* how you feel about that choice allow your authentic self to feel the energy of blossoming expansion or the energy of contracting stagnation.

When you align your choices with what you know is right and true for you, you nourish and expand your soul from a more joyful place, and you get to enjoy the benefits of the results you create.

Our resistance often reveals
previously held wounds
ready to be healed.

thirty-three

Whatever triggers you is an invitation to heal a wound that is within you. The greater the intensity of emotion you feel, the deeper the wound. The deeper the wound, the greater the growth you will experience as you choose to look within and heal.

Successful people create success, freedom and happiness from transforming previously held stories and wounds in life and not allowing new ones to take hold.

We are calling forth the
very things we are experiencing.

thirty-four

It's often hard to imagine that the majority of what is showing up in our lives is what we are *actually* co-creating. It can be challenging to see that when we have negative experiences like being fired or injured, we may have something to do with that creation. We think, "That's impossible! Why would I ever create this or that?" Yet, when you are willing to look at how you are consistently thinking, feeling and acting, you can begin to easily see where you put the majority of your focused attention by noticing the results that manifest.

Successful people know that to create the life of their dreams, they need to consistently focus on what they are wanting to create—and nothing else. They understand that *acting as if their dreams have already manifested* is an important part of creating their desired life. Instead of focusing on what they don't want, they turn their attention to what they *want* to create.

Speak only positively about
yourself and what you desire.

thirty-five

We are not born thinking or speaking negatively about ourselves or our future. Negative self-talk begins when we allow other people's opinions, beliefs and criticisms to live within our thought processes and body. If we draw from those negative and integrated experiences as continued proof that something is wrong with us, we miss seeing the truth of who we are: *Amazing soul beings here to enjoy the contrast of life, learn to expand consciousness through our experiences, and create joy and freedom for ourselves.*

Creating a successful life that feels integrated with joy, love and freedom comes from censoring any negative conversation we have about ourselves, whether those thoughts are within our mind or in conversations with others. Successful people choose to reframe and redirect their conversations by focusing on their positive aspects and what they want.

You have never been and
will never be alone.

thirty-six

Everyone experiences feelings of loneliness, separation and isolation. Often these feelings appear at times where we're feeling overwhelmed, afraid or lost. Our inner critical voice often creates these feelings of separation with the consistent bombardment of negative chatter. Learning to extinguish the negative critical voice is the first step in re-creating connection and dissolving the sense of isolation.

Successful people understand the irony of taking time to be alone so that they don't feel alone. By cultivating a practice of prayer, quiet time or meditation, they create a conscious connection and remember that they are never alone. They also free themselves from times of suffering and feeling isolated by reaching out to friends, family, colleagues, mentors, counselors or coaches for support.

Creating a daily practice of stillness and asking for support will gift you the understanding, the knowing and the remembering *you are never alone.*

You were never meant
to *do this* alone—ask for help.

thirty-seven

Within the depths of our being, we know that anything is possible. Within the energy of possibility, we also know that multiple solutions and choices exist. Asking for help is a gift to yourself and others, demonstrating that we are not alone and will never be alone.

Asking for help and then expecting answers, inspiration and support to arrive are essential for creating a successful life. Successful people learn to ask for help *and* pay attention to all the unique ways support can show up, whether that is directly from Spirit or through other people.

It is better to give *and* to receive.

thirty-eight

Creating financial freedom is often limited because of our stuck energy within our ability to receive.

Giving and receiving go hand in hand: One does not happen without the other, and, as we are so often told, one is not better than the other.

Successful people understand and continually dissolve limiting beliefs around the ability to receive so that they can co-create limitless possibilities with the Universe. They also are aware that there is perfect harmony in giving *and* receiving, knowing that one is not more important than the other.

♥

Stop waiting for what you *think*
is worthy of celebration; look for
something in your current moment.

thirty-nine

Daily celebration is crucial to your happiness. While most people wait until "something big" happens to celebrate and feel happy, as a result they create a lot less in life to celebrate and can feel greater apathy towards life, instead of happiness.

Happy, successful people know that in practicing celebration daily— whether it's celebrating in the moment or celebrating as they review their day, they are creating more experiences to celebrate in their future.

Being successful requires living in a space of *celebrating it all*.

Your words have
power and substance.

forty

What you speak, write or think makes a difference in what you create in your life. Your most private thoughts—what you have come to believe is true for you—are often the most powerful in what shows up along your journey.

Successful people know that despite what they say to others or how they act, what lives inside of them matters most in the results they create. They learn to investigate and eliminate any thoughts, speech and actions that are not in alignment with what they want to create.

Learn to align your inner voice with your outer action and speech.

Intuition is the portal
to everything you want.

forty-one

Successful people use their intuition. Not all successful people label the gift of hearing, seeing, feeling and knowing as *intuition*, but they utilize it nonetheless. Intuition is the human version of a car's GPS system — a living map.

The greatest of the great inventors, writers, philosophers, doctors, athletes, leaders and healers co-created and allowed streams of intuitive consciousness to permeate their everyday questions and guide their hands, mouths and pens. Those we deem the greatest were great to the extent that they utilized their own portal of intuition.

Using your intuition allows what is great within you to be shared with the world.

The most powerful combination
of words you can use is
"I AM."

forty-two

Some individual words as well as combinations of words are more powerful and harmonious than others. The most powerful combination of words you can use is "I AM" and anything following these words. "I" represents the true essence of your very being as an individual extension of creative Divine energy, while "AM" represents the command or action that is being summoned by that creative Divine energy to take action with whatever words follow "I AM."

Successful people understand that their words have substantial power, and in this power of the "I AM," they understand that whatever they are commanding most often will show up in the results they create. They understand that the Universe delivers what follows "I AM" consistently.

Always be mindful of what words follow your "I AM."

Trust that you innately
know what to do.
And do it!

forty-three

One of the greatest gifts you can give yourself as well as others is to honor what is right and true for *you*. Your fearful and critical ego has its own version of what it *thinks* is right and true for you, while your wise inner voice actually *knows* what is right and true for you.

Listening to the *egoic* voice generally leads to pain and suffering, while listening to your wise inner voice will lead to a more aligned and authentic life that you can feel proud of.

Learning to discern the difference between the two voices that journey with you is key to your success. The more you learn to discern and then follow through with action based on the inspiration and direction your wise inner voice offers you, the more satisfied you will be with the successes you create.

Listen to your body's wisdom.

forty-four

Your body has a lot to say, and it is in constant communication with you about your life. Your body will remind you instantaneously when you are not speaking your truth, not listening to your intuition, disempowering yourself through the words that you speak, not pursuing your dreams, and engaging in anything you believe is not good for you.

Ignoring body communication like the warmth some people feel when they tell a lie, an ache in their stomach when they do something they actually don't want to do, or the lump or soreness in their throat when they hold back speaking their truth and sharing their feelings can create dis-ease or injury.

Creating an ongoing successful and happy life will involve paying close attention to how your body feels throughout each day and taking action based on what is right and true for you.

Bonus Section

Excerpt from

It's OK to be Spiritual AND Wealthy:
19 Essential Keys for Living a Joyful,
Prosperous & Abundant Life

Deborah "Atianne" Wilson

We Are Always Creating

It is your Divine birthright to create anything you want in your earthly life. You are the outer-most directive expression of Co-Creative Energy. YOU are here to play and grow and expand that energy.

You get to play out this life,
***your* life, any way you want.**

Even as a little girl, I knew that if I wanted something, I could make it happen. Children are very clear about their ability to co-create and manifest their ideas and desires into reality. Each of us did this with ease and grace until someone told us we couldn't. Then, for some of us, life got a bit bumpy as we took on other people's beliefs, rather than believing in ourselves and our own abilities.

Just for a moment, remember a time when you really wanted something to happen, and you were able to bring it into your life. You were clear about what you wanted, you thought about it a lot, and you imagined what it was like to have it. In other words, you were already experiencing it in the NOW. The feelings associated with this experience were good feelings, bringing you a sense of joy and well-being.

Now, remember a time when you worried about something happening that you didn't want, and it happened anyway. Just like the "positive" experience, you were clear about what you didn't want, you thought about it a lot, and you imagined what it would be like if it were to happen. In other words, you were experiencing it in the NOW, and your thoughts created anxious feelings, which brought a sense of fear and anxiety.

Both of these scenarios exist because this field of Co-Creative Energy is operating *every* second of *every* minute of *every* hour of *every* day of *every* week of *every* month of *every* year, and this Energy never *ever* takes a break or a holiday. You are receiving *exactly* what you are extending energetically.

Whether you are aware of or believe in this Co-Creative Energy, it's doing its thing. However, when you are aware, and when you allow yourself to become playful with this knowing and your own power to create, then you can become the conscious, joyful co-creator of your own destiny.

Ask, Listen and Take Guided Action

One of my very favorite quotes comes from Michael Bernard Beckwith who said, "You can't hide your secret thoughts because they show up as your life." These thoughts are both conscious and subconscious beliefs that are directing your life. Both can be changed in any direction that you desire.

In my life, positive change happens when I take action based on my intuitive guidance. First, I ask what I call *clarifying questions*. Then, I *listen* for the answers and take what I call *guided action*. I trust that my questions are always answered, and it is up to me to be unattached to what the answer is or how it shows up.

What I love about honoring my intuition and the spirit world is that I get what I call *insider information*. At any moment I can access wisdom and information that allow me to be happier, healthier and wealthier in my personal life, while also using this insider information to guide, inspire and show others how to do the same.

One morning I was thinking about how so many beliefs about money, spirituality and relationships keep people stuck in a vicious cycle of victimization. So, I asked the angelic realm what I needed to know about these limiting beliefs. True to angelic form, they offered a perspective and definition larger than I expected:

**True Spiritual Wealth comes from knowing
that your thoughts create your reality.**

Spiritual AND Wealthy people understand this truth and are mindful of what they say, how they feel and what they do. They understand that how they spend their time and with whom makes a difference in the life that they are co-creating.

This information and initial awareness can be a bit shocking for most people at first. It takes courage to reconcile that ultimately each and every one of us is responsible for the choices we make in our thoughts, feelings and actions.

Once we awaken to this awareness, we can then consciously focus our Co-Creative Energy in amazing and thrilling ways that often seem magical. More importantly, we can create a life we love.

My Own Powerful Transformation

At one point in my life, I was extremely ill. Within a seven-year period, I was diagnosed with and treated for cancer and then an autoimmune disorder that turned out to be far more physically and emotionally life-changing than the cancer had ever been. My doctor told me that there was no cure and that the painful, debilitating and life-altering level of dis-ease that I was experiencing would stay the same or get worse.

During one of my most miserable days experiencing this dis-ease, I lay in bed, freezing. I was unable to sustain a normal body temperature, even though I was fully clothed and covered with multiple blankets and a heating pad. Ironically, this day would become one of my most life-defining days and moments.

I remember quietly saying, "This house is so cold."

Instantly, I heard a voice so clearly and beautifully say, "You need to leave this house."

I asked, "Why?"

I then heard, "Because there is a better life waiting for you."

I asked, "When?"

I then heard, "Less than two years."

And that was it. The conversation ended.

The room continued to hold a palpable presence and familiar stillness, which was infused with the comfort of hope and love—and a sense of normalcy. I felt profound clarity, and I felt safe.

As I wondered about the words spoken, "There's a better life waiting for you," I imagined that if a better life was waiting for me, *then it had to be better than what I was currently experiencing*.

Then, intuitively I knew that if my body "could get into this mess," then my body "could also get out of this mess." I was clear that if I expected my health and my life at that time to be different, it was going to be up to me to make it happen. That knowledge and awareness of personal responsibility changed my life forever.

Within the next two years, I shifted my diet, did transformational work, moved my family out of state, ended a 23-year-old relationship and changed careers. *My positive changes required more than just thinking positively*; they required my asking Spirit for help, listening to the guidance given, and taking action that sometimes felt uncomfortable and terrifying. I healed my body, and the positive shifts rippled throughout every area of my life.

> **When you change your attitude and actions, you**
> **can quickly create a positive impact on your life.**
> **In fact, when each of us positively changes our**
> **own life, we also positively affect those around us.**

When we consciously connect to Spirit, we experience a dramatic increase in synchronistic events or what many people call *coincidences*. I personally don't believe in coincidences because they imply randomness without cause and effect, which is in complete contrast to what was given to me by the very definition of "True Spiritual Wealth," the essence of Spiritual Law.

Everything that makes itself known in your life is perfectly aligned and matches your Co-Creative Energy. What we think and feel about what shows up gifts us a great opportunity to get curious and notice whether we are happy with our results. If we are not happy with the results in our life, we can choose differently, creating *new agreements* with ourselves and others.

Your life can then become what it was truly meant to be, an expression of what you want and desire as a direct result of your conscious Co-Creative Energy.

Co-Creative Energy Has Many Names

Each religion and group of individuals that allow a space for what they believe to be sacred have a name for this energy. "IT" has been called the Universe, Divine, Source, God, Oneness, Quantum Field, Unconditional Love, Infinity and so on. So far, I've referenced "IT" in several ways and will continue to do so in this book as a way of supporting the collective healing and understanding that there are specific words that call each of us to awaken. While one person may resonate with *God*, another may resonate with *Source*.

Deep healing occurs when we realize that vibrationally there is no "wrong" word for this Co-Creative Energy. Any word that awakens *your* inner knowing can only be "right."

So, it doesn't matter what you call "IT." From the angelic perspective, "it matters not what you call us, just that you do." We can label "IT" in many creative ways, yet it does not change the truth: "IT" just is and always will be.

Let's consider gravity. You can call it by any name, you can believe in its existence or not, yet the truth remains the same: it just is. Having awareness and an appreciation of the Law of Gravity, for example, can and does have a direct effect on your life. Gravity, just like Co-Creative Energy, is doing its thing, despite our beliefs about it or what we call it or how we name it.

Open to Your True Spiritual Wealth

The more you open your awareness to your "True Spiritual Wealth," the wealthier you become, not only from a spiritual standpoint but also from a material one:

True Material Wealth comes from
feeling joyful about what you created.

From this angelic perspective, we are invited to open up and go beyond our current collective and individual beliefs about what "Material Wealth" really means. Like anything in our lives, the meaning, value and beliefs we place on something deem it "positive" or "negative."

"Material" then becomes everything that you have and experience in your life, which has come into form from your consistent thoughts and feelings. Regardless of *what you have, how you feel about what you have* becomes the true mechanism for measuring your Material Wealth.

The essence of True Material Wealth is not saying that you should feel joyful about something like cancer. Rather, as we evaluate our emotional state, based on this definition, we have an opportunity to change the direction of our lives when we realize that what we have created is not feeling joyful to us and that we can make new choices.

I was not happy about having cancer, nor was I joyful about the prognosis or effects of the autoimmune dis-ease. However, I realized that I could choose to get very curious about my life and take responsibility for how it was playing out at that time.

I actually was so irritated at the doctor and his bleak opinion of how things were going to go for me that I got clear very quickly that I was going to prove him wrong. Anger became a positive aspect of my initial motivation, and getting well became a place of determination and excitement. It turned out he was the perfect doctor for me and for my healing because he guided me in a synchronistic way to heal myself.

I got curious and asked Spirit to show me how I was going to return to health. Then, I paid attention to everything and everyone that even hinted at being answers to my question. As I paid attention to the ideas and inspirations that I attracted, I took action. I expected to heal, saw myself healed, and felt what it would be like to return to health.

If you're not experiencing joy, direct *only* positive thoughts and feelings toward any outcome you desire. As you learn to create more experiences that feel joyful, and focus more of your attention on joy and *feeling* joy, you will increase your ability to attract and manifest more joyful outcomes. Starting where you are right now, you can easily evaluate from the angelic perspective how Spiritual AND Wealthy you are.

It doesn't matter what you have; it only matters how you *feel* about what you have.

Deborah "Atianne" Wilson
The Intuitive Spiritual AND Wealth Coach

About the Author

Everything that has shifted, healed and transformed in Deborah "Atianne" Wilson's life has come from the foundational knowledge that *it all matters—we all matter*. From her gift of spiritual neutrality through the portal of her intuitive abilities, she was invited to change her thoughts, emotions and every area of her life.

Deborah has been exploring questions many of us have asked as we navigate and investigate this wild and often intense experience we call life. Her initial questions like "Why me?" blossomed along her 32 years of inner spiritual inquiry to reveal higher perspectives like "What wants to be revealed now?" or "How can I see this through the eyes of Love?"

Abuse, abandonment, rejection, death, divorce, dis-ease, infertility and financial fears invited Deborah to shift from a place of depression, physical pain and *egoic* misunderstanding to extraordinary places of peace, empowerment, personal responsibility, healing, joy, authenticity and Love.

As a contemporary spiritual teacher, Deborah's passion is to offer practical application for ancient spiritual wisdom. As an author, speaker and mentor of prosperous living, she has created products and services that meet people at the level that they are ready to invest in themselves, from free offerings like her weekly Spiritual AND Wealthy radio show to platinum-level coaching programs. When people are ready to make the necessary shifts to get where they need and want to be in this life, Deborah is excited and able to assist clients worldwide.

Although a native Californian, she currently lives in Boulder, Colorado, savoring motherhood, the beauty of the mountains and all the playful shenanigans that come with living a Spiritual AND Wealthy life.

Notes

Notes

Share the Love!

How is this book positively making a difference for you? I would love to hear what is creating a change within you and touching your heart from connecting in with my passionate work.

I invite you to share your letters or e-mail messages with me:

Deborah "Atianne" Wilson
Angels And Prosperity
PO Box 7119
Boulder, CO 80306

Deborah@angelsandprosperity.com

Feel the Love

Please visit my websites to see my latest offerings and programs and learn how I can support you to create a life of freedom.

www.angelsandprosperity.com
www.onenessbecomesyou.com

Booking Deborah & Quantity Discounts

Interested in booking Deborah to speak
at your next event or program?

Quantity discounts for her books, home-study course or
Oneness Becomes You™ music are available.

Contact our office at
774-31A-NGEL

www.ingramcontent.com/pod-product-compliance
Lightning Source LLC
Chambersburg PA
CBHW030156070426
42447CB00031B/549